The best guide to intermittent fasting for women

Author

Camille F. Barbosa

Introduction

It's challenging to lose weight in your fifties. You can't eat the same diet as people in their twenties and expect to feel fine the next day. It's even risky!

Let me tell you something: there is another, healthier, and more long-term way to lose weight. Intermittent fasting is the most effective way to lose weight. You may have heard about it on the internet. Many people have reported health benefits as well as weight loss as a result of taking this supplement.

This book will show you how intermittent fasting is both natural and beneficial to your health. It will also show you how to do it and what other weight-loss strategies you can employ. Let's get this party started, shall we?

The Science of Intermittent Fasting

Intermittent fasting can be described as a way to eat, rather than a diet. You don't have to change what you eat in many cases. This name is a result of the fact that you must alternate between fasting and eating.

Intermittent fasting's greatest advantage is its flexibility. Your fasting times can be customized to suit your needs. You can customize some of the most popular fasting patterns, such as 16/8, 5/2 and OMAD.

Intermittent fasting doesn't require you to keep track of your macronutrients or calories. You will learn what foods you should avoid and when to eat fast.

Intermittent fasting is a popular way to reduce body fat. This diet trend has many health benefits, including better metabolic health, increased longevity, stronger immune system, and weight loss.

Intermittent fasting is often viewed as unhealthy and unnatural. How healthy is it to skip meals? It may sound counterintuitive but it is important to remember that every diet revolves around eating less and moving more. Intermittent fasting is much easier than you might think. Many people report better results than other diets.

History of Intermittent Fasting

As ancient hunter-gathers, our ancestors didn't have as many options or the ability to preserve food for long periods of time. They had to live with what was available. Vegetables and fruits were never very filling and were also not readily available year-round. It was also hard to hunt down animals and their meats lasted much less. Humans had to choose between long periods of starvation and feasting. This was before agriculture was discovered.

What does this mean for us? One, the body evolved over thousands to conserve energy from the food it eats. However, being energy efficient comes with a price. Your body thinks it is living in an age of food scarcity. Therefore, whenever you eat, you body will try to store as much energy as possible as fat so that you are prepared for when there is no food. You will only get wider as your body will not allow it to. It is best to fast from time to time to allow your body to lose some extra energy.

Things to Consider

As we have already discussed, intermittent fasting offers many benefits. It isn't as simple as you might think. Here are some things to remember.

You can best do intermittent fasting if you get enough fluid. Your body can store energy efficiently, but it doesn't have the same efficiency for fluid.

Drink plenty of water to replenish your body's fluids. You are likely already dehydrated if you feel thirsty. Your body is most dehydrated when you drink 500ml to 1l of water right after you

wake up. You can have unsweetened tea and coffee throughout the day, but only with minimal sugar or milk.

Water has many important benefits for our health. Water can aid in maintaining a healthy blood level, which means that your skin and organs will be healthier and more able to fight diseases and inflammation.

On average, you need to drink three liters per day. Two of these can be obtained from water and the rest from food. If you need to detoxify or if your body loses a lot of fluid due to exercise, diarrhea, or other reasons, you may need to drink even more. You may need to drink up to four liters per day in this case. Four is the ideal number for fasting. This is because you have to compensate for any food you don't eat. The body will eliminate the extra fluid naturally, so you don't need to worry about drinking too much water. Drinking a little bit too much water can allow your body to flush out toxins. Drink a lot of water and drink it often.

People may find it hard to drink enough water and feel terrible from dehydration. If you find it difficult to drink enough water, keep a glass of water close by. You will soon become a regular drinker. Then you will feel better.

We will discuss what you'll eat later. You can eat the same food as before. To create a calorie deficit, you just need to adjust the amount. This can be achieved by restricting your intake during a certain time period.

You should also ensure that you have enough energy. Intermittent fasting and dieting are two ways to quickly lose weight. This is fundamentally incorrect. It is wrong. You want to feel great, which means that you must have enough energy to keep yourself going. You can eat as normal and fast when you want to lose weight.

You should eat a balanced diet. This means you won't have to give up your favorite steak, hamburger, or pie. You can just add other foods to make your meal more balanced. This will allow you to get all the nutrition your body needs, while still satisfying your tastebuds.

Women need to listen to their bodies, as they may have a more specific need. Sometimes they may not be able to follow a particular fasting schedule for one reason or the other. They will need to adapt the fasting plan to be both easy for women and newcomers. There is one rule for intermittent fasting. You can skip one or more meals and still eat normal without trying to make up for it.

Fasting is easy. There are times when you should and shouldn't eat. You could even skip breakfast and practice intermittent fasting (16/8). It's that simple. Fasting is beneficial, but you must have your stomach empty and intestine empty before you can reap its benefits. Fasting must last for at least 24 hours without eating. This is to ensure that your stomach and intestine can process the last meal before you stop eating. Selfcleaning and healing can only then begin.

It takes between 12 and 14 hours for this to occur. There are many types of intermittent fasting you can try, so you can find what works best for you. Listen to your body and try different fasting methods until you find the one that works best for you.

There are three main types of intermittent fasting. Intermittent fasting is flexible because it primarily addresses when and how often you should eat. You can create your own routine if you wish, provided that you allow enough time for your body to cleanse itself. This means that your routine should include at most 12 hours of fasting.

How do you start intermittent fasting when you're over 50?

Intermittent fasting for people over 50 is not as easy as it sounds. Your metabolism is the most important thing. As you age, your metabolism slows down. Your metabolism will slow down and your body will require fewer calories to sustain itself. This means that you can cut calories in a greater amount than in your 20s.

You might try fast-mimicking if you're just getting started and don't know if intermittent is right for you. Fast mimicking allows you to consume a limited amount of calories while still enjoying the benefits of fasting.

Fasting for five days is a good idea. You need to limit your intake of carbs, protein, and calories while limiting your intake of fat. You should limit your calories to 40 percent of your usual intake.

You would still get enough nutrients and electrolytes.

Fast mimicking is much easier than intermittent fasting and traditional fasting. How do you fast mimic?

Simultaneous fasting is a way to trick your body into believing you are fasting. This trick tricks your body into thinking you are fasting. You can then reap all the benefits of fasting, while still nourishing your body.

It doesn't take too much time. It is usually only necessary to do this for between 3-7 days. Before you do anything, consult your doctor.

Begin by asking yourself if you're interested in keeping track of your fasting results. You might also consider doing lab tests prior to and after your fast, such as measuring biomarkers like blood glucose, ketones and weight change.

It is also helpful to create an environment that encourages your fasting efforts. You can do so by:

Letting those you plan on seeing while you are fasting know what you are doing and why it is important for you, so you can get emotional support.

Taking away temptations such as snacks at home and work. You will feel more tired if you sleep more. Plan for some exercise every day. But, stick to light, easy exercises.

Creating a meal plan so you know what you put into your body.

Your first fasting-mimicking meal should be 50 percent of your daily calories, as opposed to the 40 percent we discussed earlier. This will allow your body to adjust.

You can gradually increase your intake from the second to the fifth day. It is important to eat food that your body can easily

digest.

ProLon FMD is a prepackaged fast-mimimating diet that includes all the food you need for five days. However, it doesn't mean you have to spend a lot of money to get it. Make sure to match the numbers and plan your meals accordingly. These are the numbers:

First day: 34 percent carbs, 10 percent protein, and 56 percent fat.
Rest of the days: 47 percent carbohydrates, 9 percent protein and 44 percent fat.

Notice: The percentage is a fraction of your daily calorie intake. For the first day, it is 1,000kcal for women and 1,250kcal per day for men. It is 800kcal and 1,000kcal respectively for the rest of the days.

You can also drink a cup of tea or black coffee every day if you like tea or coffee. You should avoid adding creams or sugar to your coffee.

The 30-Day Weight-Loss Program is a 30-day weight-loss program designed to help people lose weight quickly

This chapter will provide you a 30-day weight reduction plan to help you transition to intermittent fasting. After reading this chapter, you should be comfortable fasting. This strategy may be tweaked to meet your specific requirements. We'll presume you've previously tried fasting-mimicking since it's quite simple for people in their 50s. It's an excellent method of weight loss.

The first week

We're going to use the 16/8 approach first. This indicates that the eating window of 8 hours and the fasting window of 16 hours are the same. This is a wonderful choice for beginners since you can cut out a lot of the work by missing breakfast. This is why it is critical to begin here.

Fasting could be challenging for some individuals. If that's you, no problem! Alternate 16/8 diets enable you to fast for 12 hours and then eat for the remainder of the day. You may eat whenever you like between the hours of 7 a.m. and 7 p.m. All you have to do is choose a 12-hour window that works for you and stick to it. If you start eating at 7 a.m., you should be finished by 7 p.m. Coffee and other drinks are included in this category. Between the hours of 7 p.m. and 7 a.m., you must consume nothing except water. Given that you only sleep for around two-thirds of your fasting period, the remaining four hours shouldn't be too problematic.

For the first week, stick to the 16/8 modified fasting pattern.

Second week

By this time, your body should be used to fasting for the second time. Dinner must be had no later than three hours before bedtime during the second week. This is necessary because your stomach must be empty before your body can rest. This will lead to a more peaceful night's sleep and a more consistent sleeping pattern. If there is still food in your stomach, your body will function. You may feel agitated as a result.

By ceasing eating after 7 p.m., you may align both your brain's and your body's internal clocks. Allowing your stomach to empty while standing can help to realign your brain and body. It's a good rule of thumb to stop eating 3-4 hours before night to ensure your stomach is empty before you go to sleep. Before you go on, give it at least two weeks. If you've been doing it from the beginning, you may continue for two more weeks. It's critical to synchronize your circadian cycles over the following two weeks before continuing.

If you can't stop eating late at night, you may make it more difficult for yourself. This may be accomplished by stocking your refrigerator with enough food to last a few days and removing any snacks. This will prevent you from snacking whenever the need arises. Even if you don't have any food, the sight of potato chips may make you feel satisfied. Even if pizza is your favorite snack, the knowledge that you can contact Pizza Hut at any time will keep you from consuming too many. When temptations are there, it is much simpler to resist them.

Snacking is challenging.

the third week
You may now let your stomach empty before going to bed after your body has accustomed to the 12-hour alternating fasting/feeding cycle. It's time to start eating less. You'll only be able to eat for 8 to 9 hours, with the remainder of the time devoted to fasting. This is the 16/8 approach we discussed before, and it should be used for a week.

the fourth week

We've progressed to the OMAD/ESE technique, sometimes known as the 24-hour fast, which is more difficult. It's time to start fasting 24 hours a week after your body has become used to 16 hours of fasting every day. Fasting from breakfast to lunch, supper to dinner, or even lunch to dinner is possible. If your body isn't attuned, you might anticipate to be hungry, particularly around meals. Remember that hunger comes in waves that last no more than 10 minutes. You should be alright if you can retain your cool or divert your attention.

Fast for 24 hours, then use the 16/8 technique for the rest of the week. This will help you build up your tolerance for fasting on a regular basis or for extended periods of time. Fasting for up to 72 hours is possible, although it is not advised.

Once you've mastered this fasting approach, you can either mix in the ESE/OMAD with the 16/8 or stick to the 16/8 method entirely.

Consider the following activities:
There are a few other ways to improve intermittent fasting.

Exercising

Why should you engage in physical activity? Intermittent fasting is simple to do, so you can get some exercise in as well.

In your 50s, it's especially important to keep your muscles in shape. You've lost a lot of muscle mass as you've gotten older. Maintaining any muscle that you do have becomes even more important as a result. Regular exercise will push you past your limits, allowing you to accomplish more than the average person your age. This is frequently the deciding factor as to whether or not to stay outside. Exercise can also help you burn fat, so unless you have a medical condition, you don't have to skip it.

The best exercise for you is the one that meets your needs, similar to intermittent fasting. Lightweight or aerobic exercise are best for your age because they don't put your body under too much stress. Swimming, cycling, and running are all excellent alternatives.

A warm-up, actual training, and cool-down phase should all be included in a workout. Warm-up is when your muscles are warmed up. This can be accomplished by gently moving your arms and legs in preparation for more vigorous movements later. Warm up for ten to fifteen minutes. It should take you 30 minutes to complete your workout. During the cooldown phase, you should relax your muscles for 10 to 15 minutes.

Fruits should be consumed in moderation.

Fruit (not juice) is a good snack option if you're hungry. You'll be fuller for longer and your liver's glycogen will be replenished. When the liver is depleted by long fasts, it sends a signal to the brain to cause hunger.

You can eat some fruits to satisfy your hunger pangs if you are fasting. You can also help your body return to anabolic mode by replenishing your liver glycogen.

When is the best time to indulge in this nutritious treat? It's best to eat it on an empty stomach, especially if you're low on carbs. Any carbohydrate you consume will go straight to your liver's glycogen stores as a result of this. This store will be depleted if you eat a large, carbohydrate-rich meal. More fruits will result in the storage of fat, which is the energy from the fruits, which will result in weight gain.

We recommend that you eat a few fruits every day to avoid hunger pangs. Before lunch, dinner, and bedtime, we recommend eating an apple and a banana. Because bananas are high in glucose, they are a better choice than other fruits for replenishing muscle glycogen. Bananas also cause the release of serotonin, a hormone that helps us relax and sleep better. Potassium and magnesium are also found in bananas, which can help with digestion.

Relax your muscles and get a better night's rest.

Caffeine can be used in a number of different ways.
During a fast, coffee should probably be avoided. When you drink coffee while fasting, your brain is stimulated more. Coffee can help you get more out of fasting by stimulating your metabolism, suppressing your appetite, giving you more energy, and improving your alertness.

Caffeine should only be consumed in small doses. Caffeine's effects weaken as you consume more of it. As a result, it is less effective at curbing hunger and boosting energy levels. Drink coffee during the fasting period to get the most benefits from it. During the fasting period, two cups of black coffee are recommended. If you don't want to drink coffee while fasting, you can drink hot tea instead. Although some people dislike black coffee, it is the most effective source of caffeine. Black coffee will grow on you.

It Can Become a Way of Life

Fasting can be done for longer periods of time and can be used as a supplement to a diet. You can still benefit from fasting without making a fuss if you follow these steps:

Begin slowly and give yourself as much time as you need to adjust to fasting. It isn't designed to produce a quick result. It's a safe and effective way to shed pounds over time. It's about maintaining a normal diet while losing weight and improving your health over time.

Take your time: Rapid weight loss is neither healthy nor effective, so do not expect or force it. The majority of quick fixes are ineffective. Allow yourself to be surprised when you see how much weight you have lost after a few months of intermittent fasting.

Sleep aids hormone regulation and can help you get through a significant portion of your fasting period. On an empty stomach, this means less time running.

Drink plenty of water throughout the day, particularly if you're fasting. Every part of your body will benefit from it. Water is the most basic, least expensive, and most effective medicine there is. This is a once-in-a-lifetime chance for you and your body, so take advantage of it. Find like-minded people to fast with: Fasting in a group is much easier than fasting alone because you can support each other emotionally. Everything is infinitely more fun when done with a group of people. You can either persuade friends, family, or coworkers to join you in trying it out, or you can join an online community.

Intermittent Fasting's Do's and Don'ts

Only if you eat healthy food does intermittent fasting work. Healthy food should provide enough calories and fill you up. We will be discussing some foods you should include in your fasting diet so that you can lose weight without compromising your health.

Delectable Cuisine

Veggies: Kale, spinach, sweet potato, bell peppers, lettuce, Chinese cabbage, violet cabbage, scallions, turnip, beetroot, cauliflower, cabbage, broccoli and carrot for veggies.

Fruits to eat include acai berries, gooseberries, blueberries, strawberries, pineapple, tangerine, lime, lemon, plum, peach, tomato, cucumber, grapefruit, orange, banana, apple, and a small number of mangoes.

Protein: Eggs, tofu, beans and legumes, mushroom, fish, lean cuts of pork and beef, and chicken breast.

Dairy: Cottage cheese, homemade ricotta cheese, buttermilk, feta cheese, cheddar cheese, full-fat yogurt, and full-fat milk. Almond butter, peanut butter, sunflower butter, olive oil, rice bran oil, and edible grade coconut oil are some of the fats and oils that can be found.

Melon seeds, pumpkin seeds, sunflower seeds, macadamia, pistachios, pine nuts, pecan, almond, and walnut seeds are just a few of the nuts and seeds available. Clove, garlic powder, cardamom, star anise, allspice, chili flakes, white pepper, black pepper, cayenne pepper, turmeric, cumin, coriander, onion, ginger, garlic, oregano, rosemary, fennel, dill, mint, and cilantro are some of the herbs and spices used.

Drinks: Plain water, homemade lemonade or electrolyte, coconut water, cold-pressed juices, and freshly pressed fruit juice.

You will be spoiled for choice even if you fast, as you can see. These can be used to make delicious dishes for you as a reward for all your hard work. These are the foods you should eat.

Overall, I recommend eating a balanced and healthy diet. This list is not exhaustive. We all know what's good for us and what's not. Certain things may not be the same for everyone.

Someone trying to build muscle will need requirements than someone trying to lose weight. determine your goals and use calculators to help you figure out what you should eat to achieve them.

different nutrition It is important to

Your dietary preferences will be the same. Vegans will need a different diet to meet their nutritional needs than those who eat animal products. This will require more research depending on your current health and goals. There is no one-size fits all diet.

Bad Food

Fruits: Any fruits rich in GI such as grapes, jackfruit, pineapples, and mangoes.

Protein: Fatty cuts of beef and pork, and bacon (especially bacon) (especially bacon). Dairy products: low-fat milk, low-fat yogurt, cream cheese, and

flavored yogurt.

Fats and oils: mayonnaise, margarine, butter, vegetable oil, lard, dalda, and hemp seed oil. Wholegrains: White rice, etc. Consume it in limited quantity and always eat it with at least five other veggies in the previous list to balance it out with the GI. Processed foods: Salami, ranch dip, sausages, fries, jellies, bottled jams, etc. Drinks: Fruit and vegetable juices, soda, diet soda (it doesn't help), and energy drinks.

You don't have to eat all of the above food. You can still enjoy treats from time to time, but you should aim for at least 80 percent of what you eat to make you feel better and healthier. While fasting can give you some flexibility in your food choices, it's best to eat a balanced and healthy diet for longevity and intake of micronutrients.

Let's talk about how to design your meals so you don't lose your mind while on a diet.

What to Include in Your Meals
This is a guideline for how a meal should look to you. Five types of veggies
Three types of fruits
You can have lean protein but also some red meat every once in a while. There are plenty of plant protein such as kidney beans, seeds

and nuts.
Beans, whole pulses and lentils (if vegetarian).

A few unsalted nuts, only a few
If you are in need of some dark chocolate, you can get a piece of 80 percent .

You can also use yogurt, sour cream or fruits if you prefer sweet treats. Or, you could bake and store brownies with healthier ingredients and less sugar

Keep yourself hydrated – you limit your calorie intake, not your fluid intake; stay well hydrated as this is one of the only things that keep you going

Alternatively, you can drink three or four cups of green tea during your fasting period

These are some guidelines that will help you plan your meals. It is important to plan a healthy, delicious meal that meets all of your nutritional requirements and your personal goals. You should live a healthy, sustainable lifestyle. Based on your medical history and dietary preferences, I recommend that you conduct additional research and consult your physician. If you're vegan, I suggest you read a complete vegan nutrition guide. This will help you optimize your diet. This is true even if you love meat.

Although it may seem like a lot of work this understanding your body and why is crucial to creating a sustainable lifestyle that is long-term and sustainable is key to long-term weight loss and good health. It is definitely worth the effort. Our health is our greatest asset, as many people have stated over the centuries.

Scrambled eggs with Berries

Prep Time: 5 minutes; Cooking Time: 10
minutes; Servings: 2;
Ingredients:

Egg – 1 Egg whites - 3 Whole wheat toast - 2
slices

Vegetables (any type, any time according to your
preference like cherry tomatoes, spinach or kale)
Berries – 1 cup
Directions for oil (filled in a spray-jar):

Switch on the stove - gas or electric - and keep it
maintained at a medium flame.
Spray just enough oil in a stainless-steel pan to
cook the vegetables. Heat the oil in the pan for a
few seconds before adding them.

Keep stirring the vegetables until they soften.
Then, pour in the beaten egg and egg whites and
scramble them. While they are cooking, toast the
2 slices of bread.

Serve the scrambled eggs with the toast along
with the berries (strawberries and raspberries,
blueberries, and blueberries).

Nutritional Info: Calories: 303; Protein: 23 g;
Fat: 6 g; Net Carbs: 31 g;

Prep Time: 4 minutes; Cooking Time: 9 minutes;
Servings: 2;
Ingredients:

Diced chestnut mushrooms - 1/3 cup Medium
egg - 4 oil - 1 teaspoon Directions:

Set the grill to its highest setting and leave it to
heat up. Subsequently, in an ovenproof frying
pan, heat the oil over a medium flame.

Fry the mushrooms in the pan for 2 minutes or
until they soften. Continue to stir the mixture for
1 minute after the spinach is wilted.
Spice with a pinch of salt and black pepper after
the vegetables are cooked.

Lower the flame to pour in the beaten eggs and
let them evenly spread and cook uninterrupted
for 3 minutes – just enough time to let them set.

Put the cooked meal under the grill for 2 minutes
after spritzing it with cheese. You can either
serve it hot or cold, your choice.

Nutritional Info: Calories: 226; Protein: 22 g;
Fat: 15 g; Net Carbs: 0 g;

Prep Time: 5 minutes; Cooking Time: 5 minutes; Servings: 2; Ingredients:

Orange juice – 2 tbsp
Medium eggs– 2 Spelt bread, halved - 2 slices
Rapeseed oil– 1 tsp
For serving directions, raspberries and blueberries should be prepared with 1 2/3 cups honey:

In a wide bowl, beat the orange juice and the eggs. Then, soak both sides of the bread in the mixture for about 2 minutes.

Put a nonstick frying pan over a high flame and drizzle the rapeseed oil on it. When the pan is heated, cook the soaked bread for a few minutes without flipping it or it might break. Flip and cook the other side of the bread for 1 to 2 minutes. Top the finished French toasts with the berries and the honey.

Nutritional Info:
Calories: 197;
Fat: 10 g;
Protein: 14 g;
Net Carbs: 10

g; Fiber: 2 g;

Prep Time: 5 minutes; Cooking Time: 15 minutes; Servings: 1;
Ingredients:

1/2 cup of Old-fashioned Oats
Unsweetened Vanilla Almond Breeze (almond butter) - 1 cup Stevia, or any other
non-calorie sweetener – 2 packets Salt 2 pinches
Directions: Switch on the stove and mix all the ingredients in a non-stick pot.
Combine 1 cup of water with the mixture.
Bring the mixture to boil, then turn the heat down to simmer. Cook the oats by
gently bubbling. Continually keep stirring it until its creamy and thick. When
cooked, serve with blueberries and walnuts.

Nutritional Info:
Calories: 106; Net Carbs: 11.6 g; Fat: 3.8 g; Fiber: 3.3 g; Protein: 3.7 g;

Prep Time: 5 minutes; Blending Time: 5 minutes; Servings: 4;
Ingredients:

Seedless watermelon, cut into cubes – 8 cups

Directions: Firstly, blend the watermelon chunks with the yogurt. Mix the mint with the milk until it becomes creamy.

Nutritional Info: Calories: 143; Protein: 8.3 g; Fat: 2 g; Net Carbs: 24.9; Fiber: 1.5 g;

Prep time: 3 minutes; Cook time: 2 minutes; Servings: 2

Ingredients:

Banana – ½ Frozen blueberries - 1 Cup lemon yogurt - 1/2 cup grape juice

Honey - 1 teaspoon.
Directions:

1. Blend all ingredient

s in a blender. Blend until smooth. 2. Divide the mixture into 2 glasses. Serve as a quick breakfast. Nutritional info: Calories: 261; Fat: 2.5g; Protein: 6g; Carbs: 57g

Prep time: 3 minutes; Cook time: 2 minutes; Servings: 2

Ingredients:

Banana - 1 Strawberries frozen and sliced – 1 cup vanilla yogurt, 1 cup orange juice, 1/4 cup honey – 1 teaspoon.

Directions: Blend

all ingredients together in a blender until smooth.

Divide the mixture into 2 glasses. Serve as a quick breakfast. Nutritional Info: Calories: 248; Fat: 4g; Protein: 4g; Carbs: 50g

Prep time: 5 minutes; Cook time: 15 min; servings: 2\sIngredients:

Olive oil – 2 teaspoons.
Spinach– 10 cups.
Garlic – 2 teaspoons.
Cheese, shredded– 1 cup Eggs 2

Directions: 1. Preheat the oven to 325 F
Heat oil in a large skillet. Add 1 teaspoon. Sauté garlic and spinach in olive oil for 3-4

minutes

Mix 1/4 cup cheese with the mixture and divide it into 2 ramekins
Sprinkle one egg on each spinach mixture
Bake for 12-15 minutes
Salt and pepper to taste.
Nutritional Info:
Calories: 205.7; Fat: 13.5g; Carbs: 3.6g; Protein: 17.5g

Prep time: 5
minutes;
Cook time:
10 minutes;
Servings: 4

Ingredients:

Quinoa,
cooked – 1
cup Coconut
oil - 1
teaspoon.
Coconut
sugar - 1
teaspoon.
Berries - 1/2
cup Coconut
milk

Directions:\sI
n a saucepan
cook quinoa

Mix coconut
oil with
coconut
sugar. 3. Add
berries and
strawberries
4. Serve with

a drizzle of coconut milk
Nutritional info:

Calories: 224.7; Fat: 2.5g; Carbs: 42.8g;
Protein: 4.4g

Prep time: 5 minutes; Time to cook: 25 minutes; number of servings: 12

2 eggs, 1 cup apple sauce, 1/2 cup maple syrup

1/2 cup avocado oil, 1/2 cup vanilla essence, 1/2 cup cinnamon

1 teaspoon of baking powder a quarter teaspoon baking soda 1 cup flour (whole wheat) 1

cup fresh blueberries
Directions:
Preheat the oven to 325 degrees Fahrenheit (180 degrees Celsius).
In a bowl, mix together all of the ingredients. Blueberries should be mixed into the mixture before being placed in 12 muffin cups.
20–25 minutes in the oven
Remove and serve once you're ready.
Information about the calories: 217 calories, 3 grams of protein, 33 grams of carbohydrates, and 8

grams of fat

Sandwich with Cheesy Tuna

5 minutes to prepare; 10 minutes to cook; 4 servings

Ingredients:

4 pieces of whole wheat toast

2-5 ounces light tuna pieces (fresh is best) 2 tablespoons of low-fat mayonnaise

1 tablespoon flat-leaf parsley 2 tbsp medium-sized shallots, minced 1 teaspoon lemon juice

1/2 cup cheddar cheese, grated 1 tblsp. hot sauce

2 sliced tomatoes 1/8 teaspoon salt

Grounded pepper, to taste

Preheat the broiler while you prepare the rest of the ingredients. In a medium mixing dish, combine the tuna, shallots, and mayo. Combine the lemon juice, parsley, pepper, spicy sauce, and shallots in a large mixing bowl.

Spread 14 cup mayonnaise tuna spread over one side of each of the four toasts. 2 tablespoons shredded cheese, tomato slices

Broil the sandwiches for 3 to 5 minutes, just until the cheese becomes golden, on a baking dish lined with foil, and then serve.

Information about the calories:

198 calories; 31 micrograms of protein; 8 grams of fat

13 g of net carbs

10 minutes to prepare; 10 minutes to cook; 4 servings
Ingredients:

4 tbsp ginger, shredded Turmeric, 4 tsp large carrots, 12 wholemeal bread 80g

2-3 pinches cayenne pepper + more for serving a 4 cup (800 ml) vegetable stock
Directions:
Carrots, peeled and diced

In a blender, combine the remaining ingredients. Combine all of the ingredients in a blender until they are completely smooth. Heat until piping hot in a pan or in the microwave. Garnish with more sour cream and cayenne pepper.

Information about the calories: 223 calories; 7 grams of fat; 5 grams of protein; 20 grams of net carbs

Cooking Time: 50 minutes; Servings: 4;
Prep Time: 20 minutes
Ingredients:

4 toasted pieces of sourdough bread 3 1/2
cups diced tomatoes 3 garlic cloves,
coarsely chopped Tomato puree - 1 tbsp
Large butter beans - around 3 cups or
660g Oregano dried - A huge pinch
Onion, diced – 1 Flat-leaf Parsley, finely
chopped - 2 Tbsp Feta crumbled - 125g
Extra-virgin Olive Oil - 1 Tbsp Ground
Cinnamon - 1/4 teaspoon 1 cup, 250ml
boiling water Directions:

Preheat the oven to 180 degrees Celsius
with the fan or 160 degrees Celsius with
the gas on. After the oil has heated up,
softly sauté the onion and garlic in a
wide ovenproof frying pan, seasoning
them with salt. Cook for about 10
minutes, or until the onion turns mushy.
Pour in the tomato purée and heat for 1
minute before adding the cinnamon,
tomatoes, beans, oregano, and the hot
water. Allow it to simmer after seasoning
with salt and black pepper. For around 25
to 30 minutes, place it in the oven to
thicken and boil. Serve with sourdough
slices and crumbled feta.

Calories: 276; Fats: 10 g; Protein: 15 g;
Net Carbs: 15.9 g; Fiber: 10.5 g;
Calories: 276; Fats: 10 g; Protein: 15 g;
Fiber: 10.5 g; Calories: 276; Calories:
276; Calories: 276; Calories:

Prep Time: 15 minutes; 1 hour and 30 minutes to prepare
8 people
Ingredients:
2 large carrots, diced– 2 corn on the cobs, kernels removed– 2 large leeks, thinly sliced and trimmed Ingredients for the stock: 200g finely chopped mint and parsley - small amounts of each Ingredients for the stock: 2 Carrots, finely sliced Onions, quartered

diced leeks 1 celery stick (cut into 4 pieces) – 1 bay leaf

1 Vegetable stock cube 6 black peppercorns
Directions:

Put all of the stock ingredients, including the chicken, in a very big pot and cover with 3 liters of cool water. Bring to a simmer and cook for 1 hour or 1 hour 30 minutes after it boils. Every 20 minutes or so, scrape away any froth that has accumulated.

Remove the chicken from the stock and strain it through a sieve to remove as much fat as you can.
Return the stock to the pan after rinsing it, and cook until it has reduced to approximately 2 liters. After that, add the leeks and carrots and simmer for 10 minutes to decrease the stock.
Shred the chicken and discard the skin and bones

while the sauce simmers. Combine the shredded chicken, sweetcorn, and vermicelli noodles in a large skillet.

After adding the corn and noodles, simmer the soup for around 7 minutes to cook them. Garnish with parsley and mint and serve into dishes.

Information about the calories: 288 calories; 25 grams of protein; 9 grams of fat; 26 grams of net carbohydrates; 2 grams of fiber

5 minute prep time; 5-10 minute blend time; 6 servings
Ingredients:

2 tbsp tahini paste 2 tbsp fat garlic cloves, coarsely crushed 3 tablespoons extra-virgin olive oil + more lemon juice and zest (starting with 2 lemons) 6 tbsp Greek yogurt with coriander - 3 cups chickpeas, 3 tablespoons chickpeas, 3 tablespoons chickpeas, 3 tablespoons chickpeas, 3 tablespoons chickpeas, 3 tablespoons chick
Directions:

In a food processor, combine all of the ingredients (except the coriander) and process until smooth.

Add the coriander after heavily seasoning the hummus with spices. In a food processor, combine all of the ingredients and pulse until they are coarsely chopped.

Toss it in a bowl with a spoon and a spritz of olive oil before serving. You may also use the hummus to dip cut vegetables.

Information about the calories: Calories: 179; Protein: 7 g; Fat: 11 g; Net Carbs: 7 g; Fiber: 6 g; Total Carbs: 7 g; Total Fat: 11 g; Total Carbs: 7 g; Total Fat: 11 g; Total Carbs: 7

Prep time: 15 minutes;
1 hour and 35 minutes to prepare
Ingredients/Servings: 4
drained and diced extra-firm tofu– 28 oz 2/3 cup soy sauce (reduced-sodium)
a third cup lime juice
6 tbsp. sesame oil, lightly toasted
Directions: In a bowl, whisk together the oil, lime juice, and sauce. Combine the
tofu and the other ingredients in a large mixing bowl. Set aside for 1 hour to
marinate.
Preheat oven to 450 degrees Fahrenheit and bake for 30 minutes.
Remove the marinade from the tofu and place it on two baking pans.
Evenly distribute the pieces. Preheat oven to 350°F and bake for 20 minutes, or
until golden brown.

Info about nutrition: 163 calories, 11 grams of fat, 2 grams of carbohydrates, and 19
grams of protein

5 minutes to prepare; 20 minutes to cook; 6 servings

Ingredients:

2 cups chicken (cooked) Cream 8 oz. cheese 1 tblsp. almond flour

1 teaspoon of garlic salt
While the chicken is still hot, put it in an electric mixer. Warm leftover chicken for a few seconds if you have some.

Drop spoonful of the mixture onto parchment paper and form into nugget shapes. Preheat the oven to 350°F and bake for 13 minutes, or until golden brown and done. When it's hot, eat it up!

Info about nutrition: 150 calories, 18 grams of fat, 15 grams of protein, and 1.8 grams of carbs

Prep time: 10 minutes;
5 minutes to cook; 5 serves
Crab (1 pound) is one of the main
ingredients.
1 ripe avocado, peeled and pitted

2 tablespoons of finely chopped onion 2
tablespoons cilantro (chopped).
Salt

Pepper
Fill the Instant Pot with crab.
Place the lid on top of the canister and
set the vent to "Sealing."
Cook for 5 minutes before switching to
manual mode on the IP.
Release your pressure quickly.
Allow for some cooling time for the crab.
Discard the shells and remove the flesh
from the crabs.
In a mixing dish, mix together the
crabmeat and the other ingredients. The
ingredients should be well combined.
Refrigerate.
Cool and serve.

Info about nutrition: 149 calories, 4.7
grams of carbohydrates, 13.2 grams of
protein, and 15.3 grams of fat.

Prep time: 5 minutes; 10 minutes to prepare; 6 serves

Salmon fillets (1 1/2 pound) - 1/3 cup olive oil fresh squeezed coconut milk 2 servings powdered curry 1/4 cup chopped cilantro (2 teaspoons)

Directions:

In your instant pot, combine all ingredients. Using salt and pepper, season to taste. Stir well. Place the lid on top of the container and set the vent to "Sealing." For 10 minutes, put the IP on "Manual." Release your pressure quickly.

Info about nutrition: 470 calories; 5.6 grams of carbohydrate; 25.5 grams of protein; 39.8 grams of fat

5 minutes to prepare; 20 minutes to cook; 4 servings

1 1/4 cup pomegranate seeds - 2 avocados, peeled, pitted, and meat scooped

1 tablespoon shallots (minced) 1/4 cup extra virgin olive oil, 1 tablespoon pomegranate juice Salt

Pepper\sDirections:

Squeeze

some grapefruit to get the juice. In a basin, streusel over the avocados. Toss the salad with the grapefruit juice and the pomegranate seeds.

In a separate bowl, whisk together the olive oil, salt, and pepper, as well as the pomegranate juice. Serve with a side of salad on top. Info about nutrition:

335 calories, 18 grams of fat, 3 grams of protein, and 28

grams of
carbohydrat
es.

Arugula Dressed with Sherry Vinegar

Servings: 4; Prep Time: 15 minutes; Ingredients:

8 cups arugula, 4 tablespoons olive oil
Sherry vinegar, 4 tbsp (you could use another type).

Sunflower seeds, salted and toasted – 8 tablespoons Parmesan cheese, shredded 4 tablespoons

Directions:

In a large mixing basin, mix together the arugula, salt, oil, and vinegar. Toss together 1 teaspoon sunflower seeds and flour.

Return to the bowl and stir in the Parmesan cheese.
Serve with 1 teaspoon of the remaining seed, drizzled over top, and enjoyed.

Information about the calories: 72 calories; 2.5 grams of protein; 6.7 grams of fat; 1 gram of fiber; 0.8 grams of net carbs

10 minutes to prepare; 18 minutes to cook; 11 servings Ingredients:

2 lbs/ 907.18 g turkey ground
gluten-free and regular half-cup bread crumbs 4 tblsp lemon pepper seasoning
Whisked eggs - 2 tblsp lemon juice - 1 tblsp lemon
Directions:

Preheat oven to 176.7 degrees Celsius (350 degrees Fahrenheit). Set aside 2 baking trays that have been greased with butter or oil or that have been lined with parchment paper. Whisk the lemon and eggs together in a small mixing bowl until well combined. Mix the turkey, lemon pepper, and breadcrumbs in a separate large mixing bowl.

In the large mixing bowl, pour the lemon egg mixture. Gently fold.
With your hands, combine all ingredients. A teaspoon or a cookie scoop can be used to make meatballs.

Put 22 meatballs in each pan and cook for 17 to 20 minutes, until golden brown. Serve meatballs with lemon slices once they have finished cooking. When there are 11 servings, each person will receive at least 4 meatballs.
Information about the calories: 194 calories, 24.3 grams of protein, 10.1 grams of fat, and 3.8 grams of net carbs

15 minutes to prepare; 20 minutes to cook; 6 servings;
Ingredients:

4 teaspoons olive oil, 2 large shallots, 2 garlic cloves

1 cup non-fat Greek yogurt - 1 jalapeno pepper, cut in half and seeds removed
4 cup vegetable/chicken soup with low sodium Season to taste with salt and black
pepper.
Directions:

Over a medium flame, drizzle the oil in a large saucepan. Chop the jalapeno and
shallot in a food processor while the saucepan heats up. In the saucepan, combine
them. For about 3 minutes, keep stirring frequently.

Bring the broth to a low simmer with the zucchini. Cook for 15 to 20 minutes, until
the zucchini has softened, seasoning with salt and pepper.

Remove the pan from the heat and set it aside to cool. Then, in a blender, puree it.
Reheat the soup in the saucepan over a very low heat, then stir in the yogurt. Serve
it hot or cold, depending on your preference, after seasoning with salt and pepper.

Information about the calories: 55 calories; 5.1 grams of protein; 3 grams of fat; 7.1
grams of net carbs

10 minutes to prepare; 10 minutes to cook; 6 servings
Ingredients:

6 peeled hard-boiled eggs
1/8 teaspoon of ground black pepper

2-3 tbsp Paprika for garnishing – salt – 14 tbsp Mayonnaise

Directions:

Bisect the peeled eggs into two halves and remove the yolk. Toss the yolk in a bowl with a fork to mash it. Add the mayonnaise, mustard, salt, and pepper and stir to combine. Pour the egg yolk mixture over the egg whites to serve. add a pinch of

paprika.

Information about the calories: Calories: 84; Fat: 6.1 g; Protein: 5.7 g; Net Carbs: 0.6 g; Fiber: 0 g; Protein: 5.7 g; Net Carbs: 0.6 g; Fiber: 0 g; Calories: 84; Fat: 6.1 g; Protein: 5.7 g;

Prep Time: 15 minutes; Cooking Time: 5;\sServings: 2;\sIngredients:

Ripe avocado, diced– 1 large\sFresh cilantro, chopped roughly - 1/4 cup Zucchini, cut into 1/2-inch cubes - 1 large Ground garlic cloves - 2\sHot sauce (e.g. Tabasco - 1/2 tsp Lime juice - 2 Tbsp\sSalt – ¼ tsp\sFinely chopped onion - 1/4 cup
Directions:

Set the microwave on high power level. Then, cover the Zucchini with a damp towel in a microwave-safe dish and microwave for 4 to 5 minutes so that the zucchini becomes tender.

In a sieve, drain any water from the microwave dish and lightly squeeze the zucchini to free it of water.
Add zucchini, cilantro, avocado, lime juice, garlic, onion, salt, and hot sauce to a large bowl. Mesh everything roughly until all the ingredients are combined.
You can eat it seasoned with lemon or even spread it on bread.

Nutritional Info:\sCalories: 96; Protein: 2 g;

Fat: 8 g;\sNet Carbs: 4 g; Fiber: 4 g;

Time to prepare: 5 minutes; time to cook: 15 minutes; servings: 4

Ingredients:

1 pound Swiss chard 3 tablespoons olive oil 1 cup onion, diced
Salt
12 teaspoon oregano
3 teaspoons red wine vinegar

Directions for Salt and Pepper:

Set aside the chard after chopping it.
In an oven-safe skillet, heat the olive oil over medium heat.
Add the chopped onion, salt, and oregano to the onions and cook until soft.

Season with salt and pepper after adding the vinegar.

Info about nutrition: 132 calories; 11 g fat; 3 g protein

10 minutes
to prepare;
50 minutes
to cook; 6
servings

3 fennel
bulbs - 1
cup
crumbled
Gorgonzol
a - 1/4 cup
Panko
bread
crumbs
Salt and
pepper to
taste
1. Halve
the fennel
bulbs at
the root
end to
reduce the
longitudin
al
dimension
of the
bulbs.
In a large
pan, lay

the cut side down fennel. Fill the pot halfway with chicken broth. Allow for a 20-minute simmer over low heat. Preheat the oven to 375 degrees Fahrenheit (190 degrees Celsius). In a casserole, bake the fennel bulbs cut-side down.

Mix the Gorgonzola and bread crumbs together, then equally distribute the mixture over each

bulb.
25 minutes
in the
oven
Serve with
a pinch of
salt and
pepper.

warm.
Info about
nutrition:
75
calories, 2
grams of
fat, and 3
grams of
protein

5 minutes to prepare; 15 minutes to cook; 4 servings

Ingredients:

1 gallon water 1 tsp. kosher salt
1/2 cup chopped broccoli rabe

2 tablespoons olive oil 2 cloves minced garlic 1 teaspoon lemon juice Salt pepper 2 tablespoons parmesan cheese
Directions:

Bring a pot of water to a boil, then season with salt. Simmer for about 8 minutes over low heat. Drain and then shock with cold water to stop the bleeding. Towel dry.

In a medium-low heat pan, place the garlic and olive oil. Cut the stems of broccoli rabe in half. In a large mixing bowl, combine the olive oil and garlic. Salt & pepper to taste. On the table, place the parmesan cheese.

Calories: 81; fat: 8g; protein: 2g; calories: 81; fat: 8g; calories: 2g; calories: 2g; calories: 2g; calories: 2g; calories:

Prep time: 10 minutes; 10 minutes of cooking time; 5 servings

1 head cauliflower, halved 2 tblsp. chopped onions - 2 tblsp. beaten eggs - 1 tblsp. coconut aminos

Directions:

In the Instant Pot, add a steam rack. Fill the steam rack halfway with cauliflower florets. Top with the lid and set the vent

to
"Sealing."
The timer
will be set
to 7
minutes
after
pressing the
"Steam"
button.
Release
your
pressure
quickly.
In a food
processor,
pulse the
cauliflower
florets until
they're
smooth.
The oil
should be
sautéed.
To make
the onions
aromatic,
mix them
with the oil.
After that,
break apart
the egg.
With
coconut
aminos,
season the
cauliflower
rice. Season
with extra
salt and
pepper if

required. Info about nutrition: 108 calories; 4.3 grams of carbohydrates; 3.4 grams of protein

Prep time: 10 minutes;
6 servings; 6 minutes to prepare

6 ovaries
Pit an avocado and scrape out the flesh. 1
teaspoon minced garlic 1 tsp
1/4 teaspoon of smoked paprika 3
tablespoons cilantro (chopped).

In the Instant Pot, crack the eggs.

Close the lid and turn the vent to the
"Sealing" position.

To cook for 6 minutes, choose the
"Manual" option.
Release your pressure quickly.

Before breaking or peeling the eggs'
shells, let them cool fully.
Remove the yolk after whisking the eggs
until they are smooth. 7. In a separate
dish, whisk together the egg yolk, garlic
powder, avocado, and paprika. To taste,
season with salt and pepper.
Place the avocado-yolk mixture in the
hollow egg whites. Finish with a sprig of
cilantro.

Info about nutrition: 184 calories, 4.1
grams of carbohydrates, and 9.6 grams of

protein

Noodles made with almonds and zucchini

Cooking Time: 30-35 minutes; Servings: 4; Prep Time: 15 minutes; Prep Time: 15 minutes; Cook Time: 15 minutes; Cook Time: 15 minutes; Cook Time: 15 minutes; Cook Time
Ingredients:

14 tsp crushed red pepper flakes 1 tbsp almond flour 2 garlic cloves, ground a half teaspoon coconut oil
Using a julienne peeler, cut zucchinis into thin strips. 4 cups will result. 2 tbsp extra-virgin extra-virgin extra-virgin extra-virgin extra-virgin extra-virgin extra
fresh parsley, 1/4 cup
To taste, season with salt and black pepper.
Directions: After placing the zucchini noodles in a strainer, gently mix them with salt to coat them.

Allow for 20 to 30 minutes of resting time to drain any surplus water. Then wash them under running water, drain well, and pat them dry with paper towels.

In a hot skillet over medium-high heat, add the coconut oil. Allow for 2 minutes of melting time before adding a touch of salt and almond flour and sautéing them. Cook until golden brown, about 2 minutes, then set aside the crumbs in the pan for garnish.

Return the pan to a medium-high heat, add the zucchini noodles, and cook for 1 to 2 minutes, or until they are cooked. Reduce the heat to low and move the noodles to one side of the pan. Stir in the extra virgin olive oil, red pepper flakes, and garlic for about 20 seconds, or until aromatic.
To coat the noodles in the seasoned oil, mix and stir them. Add the parsley, salt, and black pepper once the heat has been turned off. Serve the almond flour crumbs on top of the noodle.

Information about the calories: 190 calories per serving; 3 g protein; 16 g fat

Fiber: 2 g; Net Carbs: 8 g

Lentil Curry Garam Masala

30 minutes to prepare; 6 hours to cook; 8 servings; 30 minutes to prepare; 6 hours to cook; 30 minutes to prepare; 30 minutes to cook; 6 hours to cook; 30 minutes to prepare; 30 minutes to Ingredients:

curry powder (buy premade or make it yourself) – 2 tsp powdered ginger – 1 tsp red curry paste – 3 tsp

Garlic, smashed – 1 clove Turmeric – 12 tsp 12 tablespoon cumin

10 whole and half tomatoes pureed 1/4 to 1/8 cup of coconut milk

1 teaspoon salt, or according to personal preference 1 cup red lentils - 1 onion, chopped Masala with Garam

14 teaspoons cardamom, 14 teaspoons cinnamon, 14 teaspoons nutmeg, 14 teaspoons cloves, 14 teaspoons coriander

1 teaspoon black pepper

Directions:

In the slow cooker, combine the ginger, onions, curry paste, garam masala, garlic, cumin, turmeric, and lentils (washed and rotting lentils removed) and stir well. After that, add the pureed tomatoes and a cup of water to cover the lentils.

Cook for 6 hours on low heat, covered, to soften the lentils. Just before serving, stir in the salt and coconut milk. Garnish with green onions and mint and serve on a bed of brown rice or quinoa.

Information about the calories: Calories: 199; Protein: 12 g; Fat: 2.9 g; Calories: 199; Protein: 12 g; Calories: 12 g; Calories: 12

17.4 g fiber; 17.4 g net carbs

15 minutes to prepare; 50 minutes to cook; 4
servings

Ingredients:

1 medium sliced onion - 1 sprigs of sage - 2 slices of
prosciutto (fat removed) 2 cloves minced garlic 550
g skinless organic chicken breasts 6 ounces sliced
plum tomatoes 150 milliliter dry white wine
1 teaspoon tomato purée
3 cups (225 g) halved chestnut mushrooms

1 teaspoon olive oil
a tiny handful of flat-leaf parsley (chopped)
To get the prosciutto crisp, heat the oil in a big nonstick frying pan and cook it for 2 minutes. Make sure
the oil flows back into the pan as you remove it from
the oven.

3–4 minutes in the pan, fry the garlic, onion, and
herbs. Add the chicken breast to the onion bed,
season with pepper, and cook for 5 minutes over
medium heat. At the very least, you'll have to turn it.

The chicken will be golden on both sides and the
onion will have caramelized when it is done cooking.
Remove the chicken to a platter and set aside.

Increase the heat and, after the sizzling starts, pour in
the wine, allowing it to bubble for 2 minutes to
slightly reduce the temperature. Maintain a medium

heat and add the prosciutto, followed by the tomatoes (broken with a spoon), mushrooms, and tomato purée. Pour 4 tablespoons of water into the pan as well. Cover and cook for 15 minutes. When the sauce has thickened, add the chicken and simmer for another 15 minutes, or until the chicken is cooked through.
Serve with a sprinkling of parsley.

Information about the calories: 262 calories; 38.7 grams of protein; 6.2 grams of fat; 4.2 grams of net carbs; 2.7 grams of fiber

Cooking Time: minutes; Servings: 4; Prep Time: 15 minutes

Chilli paste from Sichuan 2 cm chunk pork mince – 100 g groundnut oil– 3 tbsp tofu – 450 g garlic, minced – 3 cloves corn flour, mixed with 1 tbsp of water– 1 tsp Sichuan Chilli oil– 1 tbsp Sichuan peppercorns, ground– 12 tsp light chicken stock or water– 200 ml 6 tbsp. chopped spring onions

Directions:

After draining the tofu's moisture, cut it into 1.5cm cubes. Lightly press it with a cloth to remove any moisture. Set it aside in a dish with extremely hot water.

To make the pork crispy, pour the oil into a hot wok and fried it until it is extremely hot. Drain the oil from it using a slotted spoon.

In a wok, stir and cook the bean paste for a few minutes, or until aromatic. After that, add the black beans, ginger, and garlic. After 1 minute, add the stock/water and let it bubble away.

Mix the cornflour, water, and sauce in a pan. Toss the tofu with the spring onions and mince after draining it (to eliminate moisture).

Serve with steaming white rice and Chilli oil.

Calories: 310; Protein: 22 g; Fat: 21 g; Net
Carbs: 3 g; Fiber: 3 g; Calories: 310; Protein: 22
g; Fat: 21 g; Fiber: 3 g; Calories: 310; Calories:
310; Calories: 310; Calories

Cooking Time: 1 hour and 10 minutes; Servings: 4; Prep Time: 15 minutes; Cooking Time: 1 hour and 10 minutes

Avocado, peeled, pitted, and sliced – 1 tablespoon olive oil - 1 tsp Dijon mustard– 1 tsp Frozen salmon filets (4 oz each), thawed– 4 Grill seasoning (no salt) 1 cup Romaine lettuce, chopped – 1 tablespoon cucumber, thinly sliced Lime juice – 14 cup Stevia– 1 tsp

12 cup red onion, thinly sliced
Directions:

The grill should be preheated. After that, blot the thawed salmon fillets dry with a paper towel and season with grill seasoning and oil on both sides.

Grill for 4 to 5 minutes on each side of the salmon fillets. However, make sure they're fully cooked before serving.
In a small mixing bowl, whisk together the lime juice, Dijon mustard, salt and black pepper, stevia, and olive oil.
1 cup Romaine lettuce, red onions, 14 cup avocado, 14 cup cucumber slices, and grilled salmon should all be placed on a plate. In the same manner, prepare the other three. Drizzle the lime juice mixture over each of them before serving.

Information about the calories: 320 calories; 24 grams of protein; 21 grams of fat; 6 grams of net carbohydrates; 4 grams of fiber

7-minute prep; 20-minute cook; 4 servings

Ingredients:

Skinless and boneless chicken breasts - 114 lb. 2 teaspoons of olive oil 1 tablespoon garlic and herb seasoning mix
a pinch of salt

Directions:

Dry the chicken breasts and season both sides with salt and pepper after coating them in olive oil.
Season the chicken with garlic and herb seasoning or your preferred seasoning.
Turn on the grill and brush the grate with olive oil.
Place the chicken on the hot grate and cook until it becomes white on both sides.
Cook for a second time on the other side.
It is most likely cooked when the internal temperature reaches about 160°F.
Allow 15 minutes for the process to complete. Cut into small chunks.

Info about nutrition: 187 calories, 6 grams of fat, 32 grams of protein, and 5 grams of carbohydrates.

10 minutes to prepare; 5 minutes to cook; 2 servings

Ingredients

16 tiger shrimp, 2 tablespoons corn starch 1 teaspoon of cayenne pepper 1 teaspoon of old bay seasoning 1 teaspoon of olive oil, seasoned with salt and pepper

1, 2, 3, 4, 5, and 6 are the directions.

7. Remove the shrimp from the shell and rinse them well. Dry with a towel.
Corn starch, cayenne pepper, old bay seasoning, salt, and pepper should all be combined in a basin. Stir. Put the shrimp in a basin. Toss the shrimp in a thin coating of olive oil.
Shake off extra spice after dipping the shrimp in it. Preheat the oven to 375 degrees Fahrenheit (190 degrees Celsius). Spray a nonstick Keto cooking spray lightly on the cook basket.
Fry in the oil. Cook for 5 minutes, then shake for 2 minutes to ensure that everything is properly cooked. Arrange the dishes on a plate to serve.

Info about nutrition: 127 calories, 10 grams of fat, 3 grams of carbohydrates, and 7 grams of protein 10 minutes to prepare; 5 minutes to cook; 2 servings

Ingredients

16 tiger shrimp, 2 tablespoons corn starch 1 teaspoon of cayenne pepper 1 teaspoon of old bay seasoning 1 teaspoon of olive oil, seasoned with salt and pepper

1, 2, 3, 4, 5, and 6 are the directions.

7. Remove the shrimp from the shell and rinse them well. Dry with a towel.
Corn starch, cayenne pepper, old bay seasoning, salt, and pepper should all be

combined in a basin. Stir. Put the shrimp in a basin. Toss the shrimp in a thin coating of olive oil.

Shake off extra spice after dipping the shrimp in it. Preheat the oven to 375 degrees Fahrenheit (190 degrees Celsius). Spray a nonstick Keto cooking spray lightly on the cook basket.

Fry in the oil. Cook for 5 minutes, then shake for 2 minutes to ensure that everything is properly cooked. Arrange the dishes on a plate to serve.

Info about nutrition: 127 calories, 10 grams of fat, 3 grams of carbohydrates, and 7 grams of protein

5 minutes to prepare; 13 minutes to cook; 4 servings

Ingredients:

2 teaspoons Dijon mustard 1 tablespoon reduced-fat sour cream 12 cup sesame seeds, 2 teaspoons olive oil 4 Mahi-mahi or sole filets, wedged 1 lemon (4 oz. each)

Directions:

Rinse and dry the filets. Sour cream and mustard should be combined in a mixing dish. Apply to all sides of the fish with this mixture. To coat, roll the dough in sesame seeds.

In a large pan, heat the olive oil on medium. Pan-fry the fish for 5–8 minutes, flipping once, or until it flakes with a fork and the sesame seeds are toasted. With lemon slices, serve right away.

Info about nutrition: 282 calories, 17 grams of fat, 18 grams of protein, and 5 grams of carbohydrates

10 minutes to prepare; 15 minutes to cook; 2 servings

Ingredients

34 pound boneless skinless fresh chicken tenders Rosemary, dried – 1 teaspoon
Almond meal – 12 cup Almond flour – 12 cup Almond meal – 12 cup Almond flour
– 12 cup Almond meal – 12 cup Almond flour – 12 cup Almond meal – 12 cup
Almond flour – 2 eggs, beaten with salt and pepper

Directions

Remove the chicken tenders from the package and rinse them well before patting
them dry.
Pour almond flour in a medium mixing basin.
Whisk the eggs in a medium bowl.
Pour almond meal into a another bowl. Rosemary, salt, and pepper are all good
additions.
Toast the chicken in flour, egg, and almond meal. On a tray, arrange the ingredients.
Freeze for 5 minutes the tray.
Preheat the oven to 350 degrees Fahrenheit (180 degrees Celsius). Spray nonstick
cooking spray on the cook basket lightly.
10 minutes of cooking time for the tenders Set the temperature to 390°F and cook
for another 5 minutes, or until golden brown, when the timer goes off.
Arrange the dishes on a plate to serve. Serve with a dipping sauce of your choice on
the side.

Info about nutrition: 480 calories, 36 grams of fat, 13 grams of carbohydrates, and
26 grams of protein

Cabbage

5 minutes to prepare; 15 minutes to cook; 4 servings

Ingredients:

1 pound of mahi mahi 1 tsp. olive oil, salt, and pepper Cabbage, shredded - 2 cups
Avocado - 1 Corn tortillas - 4 2 limes (quartered)

Directions:

Add salt and pepper to the fish.
Preheat a skillet to medium-high. Heat the oil. After theoil has been applied,

Cook the fish for 3–4 minutes on each side while the pan is still hot. 1 ounce chunks
of fish, sliced or flaked
Half-cut the avocado. Remove the seed and scrape the flesh from the skin using a
spoon. 12 thick slices are cut from the avocado halves.

Warm corn tortillas in a small skillet; cook for 1 minute on each side.
Top each tortilla with a quarter of Mahi-mahi, avocado, and cabbage. Lime wedges
are optional.

Information about the calories: 251 calories, 9 grams of fat, 25 grams of protein,
and 21 grams of carbohydrates.

Strawberry Mousse that is silky smooth

15 minutes to prepare; 5 minutes to cook; 6 servings;
Ingredients:

1 cup unsweetened apple juice – 14 cup cornstarch – 1/8 teaspoon fine salt
1 2/3 cup tofu (soft silken)

2 12 cup hulled and sliced strawberries Agave nectar/honey – 1/3 cup
Directions:

A medium saucepan is used to combine apple juice, cornstarch, salt, and agave
nectar. Allow the mixture to come to a gentle simmer while stirring constantly.

Continue to cook the apple juice mixture over a moderate heat, stirring often, until it
thickens, approximately 30 seconds.

Remove the pot from the heat and let it aside to cool until it has thickened
significantly. Purée the apple juice mixture, strawberries, and tofu in a food
processor until smooth and creamy.
Place the mousse in the refrigerator for 4 hours or 1 day, divided equally amongst 6
glasses of the same length and size. It's best to serve it cold.

Information about the calories: Calories: 156; Protein: 4 g; Fat: 2 g; Net Carbs: 29
g; Fiber: 2 g; Total Carbs: 29 g; Total Fat: 2 g; Total Carbs: 29 g; Total Fat: 2 g;
Total Carbs: 29 g;

10 minutes to prepare; 6 hours to cook; 6 servings Ingredients:

8 cinnamon sticks – 4 inches orange/apple juice – 12 cup Whipped cream for serving

Place the peaches in a slow cooker in a single layer, skin side up. Place the cinnamon stick in the middle of the peaches and spritz them with the juice. Cook for 4 to 6 hours, covered. Cook them until they are as soft as you like.

Remove the cinnamon stick and serve it cold with whipped cream after it's all cooked. It may be served warm, but not with cream.

Information about the calories:
Calories: 102;
Protein: 2.3 g;
Fat: 0.6 g; Net Carbs: 21.4 g;
Fiber: 3.5 g;
Total Carbs: 21.4 g; Total Fat: 0.6 g;
Total Carbs: 21.4 g; Total Fat: 0.6 g;
Total Carbs: 21.4 g

5 minutes to prepare; 8 hours to chill 5 cup servings Ingredients:

2 cups Macadamia Nut Milk – 2 cups Orange Extract – 1 tbsp Stevia Glycerite – 2 to 2 12 tbsp Sea salt

2 tablespoons vanilla extract
In a blender, combine all ingredients.

Pour and churn the mixture in an ice cream machine. Using the ice cream maker machine, freeze the sorbet according to the manufacturer's recommendations. If you don't have an ice cream machine, transfer the sorbet to an airtight container and cover with plastic wrap. Freeze for 6 to 8 hours or overnight in the freezer.

Information about the calories: Calories: 96; Protein: 1 g; Fat: 9 g; Net Carbs: 3 g; Fiber: 0 g; Calories: 96; Protein: 1 g; Fat: 9 g; Net Carbs: 3 g; Fiber: 0 g; Calories: 9 g

10 minutes to prepare; 30 minutes to chill; 25 squares to serve Ingredients:

12 cup Creamy almond butter – 1/3 cup Maple syrup – 14 cup Coconut oil, heated – 1/3 cup Unsweetened coconut powder –

Directions:

Combine all ingredients in a small container lined with parchment paper and stir to combine. Freeze until it's firm in the refrigerator.

Remove the parchment paper from the container holding the fudge and slice the fudge into square pieces on a flat surface. Serve immediately or keep refrigerated.

Information about the calories:

Calories: 58; Protein: 1 g; Fat: 4 g; Net Carbs: 3 g; Fiber: 0 g; Calories: 58; Protein: 1 g; Fat: 4 g; Calories: 4 g; Calories: 4

g; Calories: 4 g

Cooking Time: 10 minutes; Servings: 5; Prep Time: 1 minute; Cook Time: 1 minute; Cook Time: 1 minute; Cook Time: 1 minute; Cook Time: 1 minute; Cook Time

Ingredients:

2 cups milk – 1 cup egg whites – 1 tsp vanilla 2 tablespoons corn starch– 2 teaspoons McCormick Imitation Butter Flavor– 2 teaspoons Splenda– 1/3 cup

Directions:

In a medium-sized saucepan, mix together the eggs, milk, Splenda, and corn starch. Slowly bring to a boil, stirring constantly, until the pudding thickens. Remove the skillet from the heat and stir in the vanilla and butter flavorings. Pour into chilled glasses and serve with fruits, either warm or cold.

Information about the calories: 65.3 calories; 7.6 grams of protein; 0.2 grams of fat; 9.9 grams of net carbohydrates; 0 grams of fiber

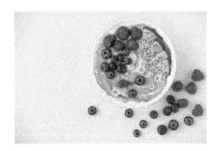

3 minutes to prepare; 17 minutes to cook; 4 servings

Ingredients:

14 cup ripe Mission figs 12 cup honey 12 cup water 12 red raspberries - 1 cup finely chopped mint leaves - 1 tablespoon

Directions:

In a microwave-safe glass bowl, combine honey and water and cook for 20 seconds on high. Remove from the oven, stir, and cool.
Place the quartered figs in the cold honey syrup. 3. In a chilled syrup, combine the raspberries and mint and let aside for 15 minutes.

Refrigerate for a few minutes
4. Place the figs and raspberries on four dessert dishes and serve.

Info about nutrition: 242 calories, 1 gram of fat, 2 gram of protein, and 62 grams of carbohydrates

6 minutes to prepare; 55 minutes to cook; 4 servings

4 cups Marsala wine Ingredients: ripe Bosc pears
Directions:

Preheat the oven to 450 degrees Fahrenheit (230 degrees Celsius).
Pour the marsala wine over the pears in a baking dish. Preheat the oven to 350°F and bake the pear slices for 20 minutes. If the dish becomes too dry, add water or additional marsala.
Cook for another 20 minutes after basting the pears with the liquid in the dish.
Bake for another 10 minutes, or until a knife placed into a pear easily passes through.
When the pears are cool enough to handle, remove them and baste them several times. With knife and fork, serve at room temperature.

Info about nutrition: 217 calories, 0.5 grams of fat, 1 gram of protein, and 31 grams of carbohydrates

5 minutes to prepare; 5 minutes to cook; 4 servings

Ingredients:

a quarter cup of red bean paste four tiny scoops vanilla ice cream 4 cups of shaved ice
flavored syrup (12 cup) for snow cones

In the bottom of four insulated paper cones or cups, spread a tablespoon of delicious red bean paste.
In each cone or cup, a dollop of vanilla ice cream is placed on top of the delicious red bean paste.

Top each cone or cup with a cup of shaved ice.
Over each shaved icemound, drizzle 2 tablespoons flavored syrup. Right away, serve.

Info about nutrition: 259 calories, 7 grams of fat, 3 grams of protein, and 48 grams of carbohydrates

10 hours to prepare; 6 hours to cook; 6 servings

Ingredients:

12-gallon milk 12 cup erythritol – 12 cup vanilla extract, pure – 1 tablespoon Yogurt starter 1 cup sour cream

Directions:

1. Fill a crockpot halfway with milk and set it on low for 3 hours. Allow the yogurt to cool before adding the vanilla, heavy cream, and erythritol.
Cook for about 3 hours on low heat.
In 1 cup of milk, whisk in the yogurt starter. Mix well in the crockpot.

Wrap the crockpot with two beachtowels and set the lid on top.
Allow 10 hours for the yogurtcultures to develop in your wrapped crockpot.

Information about the calories: 256 calories, 21 grams of fat, 6 grams of carbohydrate, and 4 grams of protein

10 minutes to prepare; 8 minutes to cook; 2 servings

Ingredients

14 CUP ALMON DRIED INGREDIENTS INGREDIENTS INGREDIENT 2
bananas, 1 teaspoon of salt
1 tblsp. sesame seed oil Cinnamon powdered 1 tblsp. of water

Directions

The banana should be peeled. Cut the vegetables into bite-size pieces using a dicer.
Toss the flour, salt, and sesame oil together in a mixing basin. 1 tbsp. water is added.
To get a smooth batter, mix everything together until it's all mixed.

Indulge in the batter with a banana. On a tray, arrange the ingredients. Freeze the tray
for 10 minutes before using.
Put parchment paper in the bottom of the fryer. Brush some oil on the paper.
Preheat the oven to 350 degrees Fahrenheit (180 degrees Celsius).

In a deep fryer, place bananas. Apply a small layer of oil to the bananas. 4 minutes on
one side, then turn and sprinkle the other side with oil. Cook for a further 4 minutes,
or until golden brown on top.

Place on a serving tray. Powdered sugar is sprinkled on top.

Info about nutrition: 242 calories, 9 grams of fat, 18 grams of carbohydrates, and 5
grams of protein

You're ready to fast occasionally at this stage. Always keep in mind that intermittent
fasting is designed to be easily integrated into your regular routine. So, do what feels
right for you and don't sweat the little stuff. Take your time, and you'll lose weight in
a healthy way.

If you follow all of the advice in this book, you should be able to reduce weight while also feeling well. I really wish you success in your work.

EFFECTS OF INTERMITTENT FASTING ON THE BODY AND BRAIN THAT MAY THWART OBESITY AND CHRONIC DISEASES

BRAIN
Improved cognitive function
Increased neurotrophic factors
Increased stress resistance
Reduced inflammation

BLOOD
Decreased insulin, IGF-1
and leptin. Increased ketones,
adiponectin and ghrelin.

HEART
Reduced resting heart rate
Reduced blood pressure
Increased stress resistance

LIVER
Increased insulin sensitivity
Ketone body production
Decreased IGF-1 levels

FAT CELLS
Lipolysis
Reduced leptin
Increased adiponectin
Reduced inflammation

INTESTINES
Reduced energy uptake
Reduced inflammation
Reduces cell proliferation

MUSCLE
Increased insulin sensitivity
Increased efficiency
Reduced inflammation